Black Beans and Mushroom Chili	
Split Pea Soup	
Pumpkin Goulash	
Beef Rolls	6
Spinach-Mushroom-Quiche	7
Chile Verde Lasagna	8
Eggplant Sauce	9
Beef Tacos	10
Chili Slow Cooker Style	11
Chicken Enchilada Slow Cooker Style	13
Overnight Oatmeal	14
Sauerkraut Soup	15
Sausage with Celery and Chicken	16
Cabbage Rolls	17
Sweet and Sour Chicken	18
Chickpea Curry	19
Roast Turkey	20
Potato Soup	21
Vegetarian Chili	22
Spinach Sauce Slow Cooker Style	23
Vegetarian Minestrone	24
Chickpea-Squash-Lentil-Stew	25
Chickpea-Eggplant-Stew	26
Bean-Barley-Soup	27
Squash Quinoa Casserole	28
Pinto Bean Mix	29

Spicy Thai Soup	*30*
Lentil-Mushroom-Stew	*31*
Mexican Spaghetti with Sauce	*32*
Chicken Soup	*33*
Slow Cooked Macaroni with Cheese	*34*
Turkey Stew Chilies	*35*
Crock Beans	*36*
Vegetable-Cheese-Soup	*37*
Vegetable-Bean-Soup	*38*
Bowtie Pasta with Sauce	*39*
Rice Casserole	*40*
Creamy Potato Soup	*41*
Slow Cooker Cassoulet	*42*
Risotto with Fennel and Barley	*43*
Slow Cooker Beans	*44*
Onion Soup	*45*
Zucchini Soup	*46*
Lentil Soup	*47*
Veggy Taco Soup	*48*
Cabbage Soup	*49*
Corn Chowder	*50*
Tofu Curry	*51*
Lima Bean Soup	*52*
Vegetarian Soup	*53*

Black Beans and Mushroom Chili

Ingredients:
500 g of black beans
1 tablespoon of extra virgin olive oil
25 g of mustard seeds
2 tablespoons of chili powder
1 ½ teaspoons of cumin
½ teaspoon of cardamom
2 onions, chopped
500 g of mushrooms, chopped
240 g of tomatillos, husk them and rinse and chop
60 ml of water
1400 ml of mushroom broth
180 g of tomato paste
2 tablespoons of minced garlic
150 g of pepper jack cheese (semi-hard cheese)
120 g of sour cream
25 g of cilantro
2 limes cut into wedges

Method:
1. Place the beans in a large pot with water and boil on medium to high heat for about an hour.
2. Drain and mix in the rest of the ingredients in a Dutch oven.
3. Cook on low to medium heat for about five hours.
4. Serve and enjoy, try with some sour cream and shredded cheese.

Nutritional Information:
Calories: 306 kcal, Fats: 10 grams, Carbohydrates: 40 grams, Protein: 18 grams

Split Pea Soup

Ingredients:
500 g of split peas
1 onion, chopped
3 carrots, chopped
3 stalks of celery, chopped
2 cloves of garlic, minced
1/8 teaspoon of pepper
1 pinch of red pepper flakes
2 liter of chicken broth

Method:
1. Chop everything up that needs to get cut and place all of the ingredients into the slow cooker.
2. Cook on high heat for about five hours, stirring every so often.
3. Serve and enjoy.

Nutritional Information:
Calories: 273 kcal, Fats: 3.4 grams, Carbohydrates: 44 grams, Protein: 17.7 grams

Pumpkin Goulash

Ingredients:
6 diced tomatoes
1 tablespoon of brown sugar
2 tablespoons of olive oil
1 onion, chopped
1 teaspoon of ginger
1 teaspoon of cinnamon
1 teaspoon of cumin
1 tablespoon of coriander
1 can of garbanzo beans
1.5 kg of fresh pumpkin, peeled and cut into small chunks
1 teaspoon of salt
1 teaspoon of cornstarch
60 ml of water

Method:
1. Peel and cut the pumpkin up.
2. Chop up everything else that needs to get cut up.
3. Place it all in the slow cooker.
4. Cook on high heat for about four hours.
5. Serve and enjoy.

Nutritional Information:
Calories: 330 kcal, Fats: 7.9 grams, Carbohydrates: 37.2 grams, Protein: 28.4 grams

Beef Rolls

Ingredients:
750 g beef brisket
2 onions, thinly sliced into rings
2 tbsp corn starch
2 tbsp cold water
270 g chili sauce
1 bay leaf
½ tsp dried thyme (crushed)
2 tbsp granular sugar substitute
1 garlic clove, minced
10 Italian Bread Rolls

Method:
1. Start by trimming off any excess fat from the beef. Place it in a 6 quart/6-7 liter slow cooker along with onions and bay leaf.

2. In a mixing bowl, mix the chili sauce with beer, sugar substitute, thyme, salt, pepper and garlic. Combine well and pour it over the meat.

3. Cover the cooker and cook on low heat for approximately 10-12 hours.

4. Once the beef is cooked, transfer it along with the onions onto a serving platter and cover it with a foil.

5. Next, in a medium sauce pan, pour the remaining mixture and stir it together with cornstarch and water. Cook the mixture for approximately 2 to 3 minutes or until the gravy thickens.

6. Serve the beef on the Italian rolls and top it off with the gravy.

Nutritional Information:
Calories; 325, Fats 8g, Carbohydrates 35g, Protein 25g

Spinach-Mushroom-Quiche

Ingredients:

Disposable liner and non stick cooking spray/cooking oil to grease
1 package (about 300 g) frozen chopped spinach, thawed and drained
4 slices bacon
1 tablespoon olive oil
150 g Portobello mushrooms; coarsely chopped
90 g sweet red pepper; chopped
150 g grated Swiss cheese
8 eggs
500 ml whole milk or half and half
2 tablespoons fresh chives; snipped
½ teaspoon salt
½ teaspoon black pepper
50 g biscuit mix

Method:

1. Line the slow cooker and spray liner with non stick spray.

2. Cook bacon until crisp; drain and crumble.

3. Heat olive oil and add mushrooms and pepper. Cook until tender then add spinach and cheese.

4. Combine eggs, milk, chives, salt, and pepper and stir into spinach mixture. Add the biscuit mixture and gently fold. Pour into slow cooker and sprinkle with prepared bacon crumbs.

5. Cook in slow cooker on low for 4 to 5 hours. If using high heat cook for 2 to 2.5 hours. Cool 15 to 30 minutes before serving.

Nutritional Information:

Calories; 431, Fats 31g, Carbohydrates 66g, Protein 25g, Sugar 2g

Chile Verde Lasagna

Ingredients:

500 g bulk breakfast sausage
150 g chopped sweet green pepper; finely chopped
1 jalapeno pepper; stemmed, seeded, and finely chopped
5 eggs beaten lightly
2 teaspoons vegetable oil
25 g green onions; sliced
¼ snipped cilantro or parsley
½ teaspoon salt
½ teaspoon cumin
9 corn tortillas; 6 inch/15 cm
200 g hard cheese of your choice (e.g. Monterey Jack Cheese); shredded
1x 480 g jar green salsa

Method:

1. Lightly coat the inside of the slow cooker with non stick cooking spray.

2. Brown sausage in skillet and drain off fat. Add the sweet pepper and jalapeno pepper to skillet and cook over medium heat for 1 minute. Transfer sausage and peppers to bowl.

3. In the same pan cook eggs in hot oil just until set; stir to break up eggs. Combine eggs with sausage and peppers. Stir in green onions, cilantro, salt, and cumin.

4. Place 3 of the tortillas in the bottom of the slow cooker; it is fine if they overlap. Put half the egg and sausage mixture in the slow cooker and sprinkle with ½ cup of the cheese.

5. Pour 2/3 of the salsa over the mixture in slow cooker. Continue layering until all tortillas, sausage mixture, and salsa are in slow cooker.

6. Cover and set to low heat for 3 to 4 hours. Let stand for 15 minute before serving. Can top with sour cream and cilantro if desired.

Nutritional Information:

Calories; 429, Fats 29g, Carbohydrates 18g, Protein 21g, Sugar 3g

Eggplant Sauce

Ingredients:

1 eggplant
2x 480 g cans diced tomatoes (or about 1 kg fresh chopped tomatoes)
180 g tomato paste
120 g sliced mushrooms; drained
60 ml red wine, dry
60 ml water
75 g onion, chopped
2 cloves of garlic, chopped
1½ teaspoon oregano
50 g olives, pitted
2 tablespoons fresh parsley; chopped
Black pepper
Parmesan cheese, shredded

Method:

1. Peel eggplant and cut into small cubes

2. In the slow cooker combine the eggplant, onion, canned tomatoes with juice, tomato paste, mushrooms, wine, water, garlic, and oregano.

3. Cover the slow cooker and allow it to cook on low heat for approximately 7 to 8 hours.

4. Add the olives and parsley.

5. Serve over cooked noodles and sprinkle with Parmesan cheese.

Nutritional Information:

Calories; 346, Fats 4g, Carbohydrates 65g, Protein 13g, Sugar 5g

Beef Tacos

Ingredients:

1.5 kg beef; trimmed and cut into 2 inch/5 cm cubes
1 large onion; sliced thin
4 chopped cloves of garlic
1 to 3 tablespoons chopped chipotle; canned in adobo sauce
1 teaspoon oregano
2 bay leaves
Pinch of salt
400 g cabbage; thinly sliced
4 radishes, halved and thinly sliced
15 g fresh cilantro
2 tablespoons lime juice
A few Corn tortillas
Toppings: sour cream, salsa, jalapenos, shredded cheese

Method:

1. In the slow cooker toss together the beef, garlic, onion, chipotles, oregano, bay leaves, and salt. (tip: add just a bit of water to bottom to avoid sticking)

2. Cook on high for 3.5 to 4 hour or on low for 7 to 8 hours.

3. Twenty minutes before meat mixture is done wrap tortillas in foil and place in 350°F/180°C oven for 5 to 10 minutes to warm.

4. While tortillas are warming and meat is finishing up, toss together the cabbage, radishes, lime juice, and ¼ teaspoon salt.

5. Transfer the meat to a bowl and shred with a fork; save the broth. Strain the liquid into the meat and stir to combine.

6. Fill tortillas with beef and slaw; top with your choice of toppings.

Nutritional Information:

Calories; 521, Fats 6g, Carbohydrates 34g, Protein 57g, Sugar 5g

Chili Slow Cooker Style

Ingredients:

500 g ground pork
500 g pork shoulder; trimmed and cut into ½ inch/1 cm cubes
300 g bell pepper; chopped
450 g chopped onion
3 minced cloves of garlic
3 tablespoons tomato paste
250 ml beer; lager style
3 tablespoons chili powder
1 tablespoon cumin
2 teaspoons oregano
¾ teaspoon black pepper
1 tomatillo, sliced
2 bay leaves
900 g plum tomatoes, chopped
450 g pinto beans, drained
220 g Mexican style tomato sauce
1 smoked ham hock
1 ½ tablespoon sugar
25 g cilantro; chopped finely
50 g green onion; chopped finely
70 g crumbled queso fresco (mexican soft cheese)
8 lime wedges

Method:
1. Brown pork in skillet and transfer to slow cooker after draining fat.
2. Brown pork should pieces in skillet until browned and transfer to slow cooker after draining fat.
3. In skill sprayed with non stick spray sauté onion and pepper for 8 minutes; stirring often. Add garlic and sauté 1 minute more. Add tomato paste and cook for 1 minute; stirring constantly. Stir in beer and continue cooking for 1 minute. Add onion mixture to slow cooker with meat.
4. Add chili powder, cumin, pepper, tomatillos, bay leaves, plum tomatoes, beans, tomato sauce, and ham hock. Cover and set slow cooker on high for 5 hours.
5. Remove bay leaves and ham hock; discard. Stir in sugar.
6. Ladle into serving cups or bowls; top with 1 tablespoon cilantro, cheese, green onions, and serve with a lime wedge.

Nutritional Information:
Calories; 357, Fats 14.4g, Carbohydrates 26g, Protein 27.7g

Chicken Enchilada Slow Cooker Style

Ingredients:
1 teaspoon canola oil
100 g onion; chopped
60 g poblano, seeded and chopped
2 minced cloves garlic
1 ½ teaspoon chipotle chili powder
450 g diced tomatoes
240 g tomato sauce, Italian seasoned
Cooking spray or cooking oil (to grease)
280 g rotisserie chicken breast; shredded
175 g frozen; white and yellow corn
450 g black beans, drained and rinsed
5 corn and flour tortillas
240 g shredded cheddar cheese; reduced fat
Cilantro sprigs

Method:
1. Using a nonstick skillet heat on medium and add oil. Add onion, pepper, and garlic; cook until tender; about 6 minutes
2. Stir in chili powder, tomatoes, and tomato sauce. Put half the tomato mixture in a blender. Remove lid of blender and let steam escape. Place a towel over blender and blend until almost smooth and pour into a bowl. Repeat process with the other half of tomato mixture.
3. Spray slow cooker with non stick cooking spray or grease with cooking oil. Spread 3 tablespoons of tomato mixture on bottom of slow cooker. Mix the remainder of tomato mixture with chicken, corn, and beans.
4. Place one tortilla on the tomato mixture in slow cooker. Cover with half of the chicken mixture. Sprinkle with cheese; about ¼ of the total amount. Top with another tortilla and repeat process until all tortillas and chicken mixture are in slow cooker.
5. Cook on low setting for 2 hours or until the cheese is melted and the edges are browned.

Nutritional Information:
Calories: 295, Fats 10.3g, Carbohydrates: 16g, Protein: 24g

Overnight Oatmeal

Ingredients:
1 liter fat-free milk
1 liter water
340 g steel-cut oats
50 g raisins
75 g dried cherries
65 g dried apricots, chopped
1 teaspoon molasses
1 teaspoon cinnamon (or pumpkin pie spice)

Method:
1. In a slow cooker combine all of the ingredients. Turn heat to low.
2. Put the lid on and cook overnight for 8 to 9 hours.
3. Spoon into bowls and serve.

Nutritional Information:
Calories: 240kcal, fat: 2.5 g; carbohydrates: 47 g; protein: 11 g protein

Sauerkraut Soup

Ingredients:
1 can (about 250 g) of mushroom soup
1 can (about 250 g) of chicken soup
600 ml of water
1 liter of chicken broth
250 g of sauerkraut
1 onion, diced
3 carrots, chopped
5 potatoes, peeled and diced
1 teaspoon of dill weed
1 teaspoon of garlic, minced
½ teaspoon of salt
½ teaspoon of pepper

Method:
1. Peel and dice the potatoes.
2. Cut the carrots and the onions.
3. Mince the garlic.
4. Combine everything into the slow cooker.
5. Put on high heat and cook for four hours.
6. Serve and enjoy.

Nutritional Information:
Calories: 387 kcal, Fats: 23.4 grams, Carbohydrates: 26.4 grams, Protein: 17.7 grams

Sausage with Celery and Chicken

Ingredients:

200 g onions; chopped
100 g celery; chopped
250 ml water
½ teaspoon Cajun season
½ teaspoon thyme dried
500 g skinless chicken (breast or thighs) cut into 1 inch/2 cm cubes
240 g sausage sliced
4 cups cooked rice
450 g canned tomatoes (diced with green chilies) undrained
1 pound medium size shrimp; peeled and deveined
1 kg cooked rice

Method:

1. Combine the first 8 ingredients in slow cooker; cover and cook on low for 6 hours.
2. Stir in shrimp and cook 10 minutes longer on low or until shrimp is done.
3. Serve over hot cooked rice and garnish with chopped green onion if desired.

Nutritional Information:

Calories; 310, Fats 8.5g, Carbohydrates 14g, Protein 30g

Cabbage Rolls

Ingredients:

12 large cabbage leaves
450 g onion; chopped
100 g instant rice; uncooked
250 g ground pork; lean
250 g pork breakfast sausage; 50% lean
¼ teaspoon black pepper
450 g can sauerkraut, shredded, drained and rinsed
½ teaspoon caraway seeds
500 ml tomato juice; low sodium
2 tablespoon brown sugar light
3 tablespoons tomato paste

Method:

1. Cook cabbage leaves in boiling water until tender; about 3 to 4 minutes.

2. Sauté onion in skillet for 5 to 7 minutes or until tender; add rice stir and let stand for 15 minutes.

3. Combine rice, pork, and pepper. Fill cabbage leaf with about ¼ of the meat mixture and turn sides in and roll. Repeat for all cabbage leaves.

4. Mix caraway seed with sauerkraut. Put half the sauerkraut mixture into bottom of slow cooker after coating with non stick spray or cooking oil. Top layer of sauerkraut with half the cabbage rolls. Repeat this step with remaining sauerkraut and cabbage rolls.

5. Combine tomato juice, brown sugar, and tomato paste with a whisk. Pour tomato juice mixture over sauerkraut and cabbage rolls. Cook on low setting for 6 hours and serve.

Nutritional Information:
Calories; 287, Fats 10.8g, Carbohydrates 12.3g, Protein 17.7g

Sweet and Sour Chicken

Ingredients:

100 g onion; chopped
30 g sugar
75 g ketchup
60 ml orange juice
3 tablespoons corn syrup
3 tablespoons cider vinegar
2 tablespoons soy sauce; low sodium
1 tablespoon grated fresh ginger
500 g skinless chicken, cubed
240 g pineapple chunks
1 bell pepper, large, cut into ¾ inch/1 cm pieces
1 red pepper, large cut into ¾ inch/1 cm pieces
600 g cooked rice

Method:

1. Combine the first 12 ingredients in a slow cooker.
2. Cook on high for 4 hours or 6 hours on low covered.
3. Serve over hot brown rice.

Nutritional Information:

Calories; 332, Fats 3.4g, Carbohydrates 7.1g, Protein 18.4g

Chickpea Curry

Ingredients:

650 g cauliflower florets, small
400 g peeled and cubed sweet potato
100 g onion; chopped
1 tablespoon curry powder
1 tablespoon brown sugar
1 tablespoon grated ginger, grated
1 ¼ teaspoon salt
2 minced garlic cloves
480 g chickpeas, drained and rinsed
450 g diced tomatoes
400 ml coconut milk, light
1 package (about 450 g) extra-firm tofu, drained
1 tablespoon canola oil
600 g cooked rice
3 tablespoons chopped cilantro, fresh

Method:

1. Combine first 11 ingredients in slow cooker and stir well. Cover and cook on low setting for 5.5 hours or until vegetables are tender.
2. Place tofu on layers of paper towels and cover with additional towels. Press down to absorb excess liquid and cut into ½ inch /1 cm cubes.
3. Heat oil in pan and cook tofu for 8 to 10 minutes or until browned. Stir into mixture in slow cooker.
4. Serve over rice and garnish with cilantro.

Nutritional Information:

Calories; 328, Fats 7g, Carbohydrates 11g, Protein 12.8g

Roast Turkey

Ingredients:

200 g onion; chopped
70 g pitted olives
30 g Julienne-cut tomato halves, sun dried
2 tablespoons lemon juice
1½ teaspoon garlic minced
1 teaspoon Greek seasoning mix
½ teaspoon salt
¼ teaspoon pepper
1 trimmed turkey breast, about 2 k
130 ml fat free chicken broth; low sodium
3 tablespoons all purpose flour
Thyme sprigs

Method:

1. Put first 9 ingredients in slow cooker. Add half of the chicken broth, cover and cook for 7 hours on low.
2. Whisk the remaining flour and remaining chicken broth and pour into slow cooker. Cook for an additional 30 minutes on low setting.

Nutritional Information:

Calories; 314, Fats 4.9g, Carbohydrates 16.2g, Protein 57g

Potato Soup

Ingredients:

3 slices bacon
100 g onion; chopped
1.5 kg potatoes; peeled and cut into ¼ inch /1 cm thick slices
120 ml water
500 ml chicken broth; low sodium and reduced fat
½ teaspoon salt
½ teaspoon black pepper
500 ml low fat milk
120 g reduced fat cheddar cheese; shredded
120 g sour cream, light
4 teaspoons chopped chives

Method:
1. Cook bacon in skillet until crisp. Remove bacon from pan and add onion to drippings. Sauté for 3 minutes.
2. Put potato slices and onion in slow cooker after coating with non stick spray. Combine water with the next three ingredients and add to slow cooker. Cover and cook on low heat for 8 hours or until potatoes are tender.
3. Mash mixture with a potato masher. Stir in milk and ¾ cup cheese. Turn heat to high and cook for 20 minutes.
4. Serve in bowls topped with sour cream, chive, and crumbled bacon.

Nutritional Information:
Calories; 259, Fats 6.4g, Carbohydrates 9g, Protein 13.2g

Vegetarian Chili

Ingredients:
450 g can of firm tofu, drained and cubed
460 g canned black beans, drained
450 g canned tomatoes, crushed
600 g onions, chopped
2 red bell peppers, seeded and chopped
2 green bell peppers, seeded and chopped
4 cloves of garlic
2 tsp ground cumin
½ tsp ground black pepper
6 tbsp chili powder
2 tbsp dried oregano
2 tsp salt
2 tbsp white vinegar, distilled
1 tbsp hot pepper sauce
120 ml olive oil, extra virgin

Method:
1. In a large skillet, heat the oil over medium heat.

2. Add the onions to it and cook until softened. Next add in the peppers, tofu and garlic and cook for approximately for ten minutes or until the vegetables start to turn brown and tender.

3. Now cook the beans in a slow cooker over low heat. Stir in all the vegetables and tomatoes and season it.

4. Cover and cook for approximately six to eight hours.

Nutritional Information:
Calories; 445, Fats 18.2g, Carbohydrates 58.2g, Protein 21.2g

Spinach Sauce Slow Cooker Style

Ingredients:
840 g tomatoes, peeled and crushed
300 g frozen spinach, chopped, thawed and drained
1 onion, chopped
20 g carrot, grated
2 ½ tbsp red pepper, crushed
5 garlic cloves, minced
180 g tomato paste
140 g mushrooms, sliced
2 tbsp dried oregano
2 tbsp salt
2 tbsp dried basil
2 bay leaves
60 ml olive oil, extra virgin

Method:
1. Combine olive oil with spinach, onion, garlic, carrots, tomato paste and mushrooms in a 5 quart/5-6 liter slow cooker.
2. Add in the salt, pepper, oregano, bay leaves and tomatoes.
3. Cover and cook for approximately 4 hours over high heat. After 4 hours are up, stir and reduce the heat to low and cook for an additional 2 hours.

Nutritional Information:
Calories; 176, Fats 8.2g, Carbohydrates 25.1g, Protein 6.6g

Vegetarian Minestrone

Ingredients:
1.5 liter vegetable broth
450 g kidney beans, drained
840 g tomatoes, crushed
900 g spinach, freshly chopped
1 onion, chopped
2 large carrots, diced
2 celery ribs, diced
1 zucchini
150 g green beans
1 tbsp parsley, minced
3 garlic cloves, minced
¾ tsp thyme, dried
1½ tsp oregano, dried
1 tsp salt
1/3 tsp ground black pepper
50 g elbow macaroni, cooked
25 g Parmesan cheese, finely grated

Method:
1. In a 6 quart/6-7 liter slow cooker, combine the vegetable broth with kidney beans, green beans, tomatoes, onion, zucchini, celery and carrot.

2. Season it with garlic, thyme, parsley, oregano, salt and black pepper.

3. Cook the minestrone on low heat for approximately 7 to 8 hours.

4. Next, stir the spinach and macaroni into the minestrone and allow it to cook for another 15 minutes or so.

5. Top it off with grated Parmesan cheese.

Nutritional Information:
Calories; 138, Fats 1.7g, Carbohydrates 25.2g, Protein 6.9g

Chickpea-Squash-Lentil-Stew

Ingredients:
150 g of chickpeas
1300 g of squash, peeled and cut into chunks
2 carrots, peeled and sliced
1 onion, chopped
200 g of red lentils
1 liter of vegetable broth
2 tablespoons of tomato paste
1 tablespoon of ginger, minced
1 ½ teaspoons of cumin
1 teaspoon of salt
¼ teaspoon of saffron
¼ teaspoon of pepper
60 ml of lime juice
75 g of peanuts, chopped
20 g of cilantro

Method:
1. Place the beans in a large crock pot and bring to a boil, cook for about an hour.
2. Drain and combine everything but the peanuts and the cilantro in the slow cooker.
3. Cook on low for about five hours.
4. Serve and enjoy, sprinkle with cilantro and peanuts.

Nutritional Information:
Calories: 294 kcal, Fats: 7 grams, Carbohydrates: 48 grams, Protein: 14 grams

Chickpea-Eggplant-Stew

Ingredients:
75 g of mushrooms
750 ml of water
2 eggplants, peeled and cut
3 tablespoons of olive oil
2 onions, sliced
6 cloves of garlic, minced
2 teaspoons of oregano
1 cinnamon stick
1 teaspoon of salt
1 teaspoon of pepper
1 bay leaf
200 g of dried chickpeas
3 tomatoes, chopped
Pinch of parsley

Method:
1. Preheat the oven to 400°F/200°C.
2. Peel and cut the eggplants, cut the mushrooms and everything else that needs to be cut.
3. Place on baking sheet and cook for 6 minutes.
4. Then transfer to the slow cooker.
5. Cook for four hours on high.
6. Remove the cinnamon stick and the bay leaf.
7. Serve and enjoy.

Nutritional Information:
Calories: 219 kcal, Fats: 7 rams, Carbohydrates: 33 grams, Protein: 9 grams

Bean-Barley-Soup

Ingredients:
1 tablespoon of olive oil
1 onion, diced
1 stalk of celery, diced
1 carrot, diced
2.2 liter of water
1 liter of vegetable broth
100 g of pearl barley
60 g of black beans
60 g of great northern beans
60 g of kidney beans
1 tablespoon of chili powder
1 teaspoon of cumin
½ teaspoon of oregano
¾ teaspoon of salt

Method:
1. Cut everything up that needs to be cut and mix it all together in the Dutch oven.
2. Put on low heat and cook for about two and a half hours.
3. Serve and enjoy.

Nutritional Information:
Calories: 205 kcal, Fats: 3 grams, Carbohydrates: 35 grams, Protein: 11 grams

Squash Quinoa Casserole

Ingredients:
360 g of tomatillos, de-husked and chopped
400 g of cherry tomatoes, chopped
1 bell pepper, chopped
50 g of chopped onion
1 tablespoon of lime juice
1 teaspoon of salt
170 g of quinoa
150 g of feta cheese
1 kg of yellow squash, sliced
2 tablespoons of oregano

Method:
1. Chop everything up that needs to get cut.
2. Place everything in the slow cooker and cook on low for four hours.
3. Serve and enjoy.

Nutritional Information:
Calories: 111 kcal, Fats: 3 grams, Carbohydrates: 18 grams, Protein: 5 grams

Pinto Bean Mix

Ingredients:
2 tablespoons of olive oil
2 carrots, sliced
1 onion, sliced
4 cloves of garlic, minced
3 tablespoons of chili powder
2 tablespoons of balsamic vinegar
200 g of pinto beans
1 red bell pepper, diced
240 g of tomato sauce
120 ml of water
2 tablespoons of soy sauce
2 tablespoons of tomato paste
400 g of green cabbage, sliced
1 zucchini, chopped
175 g of corn
3 tablespoons of honey mustard
1 tablespoon of brown sugar
1 teaspoon of salt
10 whole wheat hamburger buns

Method:
1. Cut up everything that needs to get cut up and place in slow cooker.
2. Cook on high heat for 5 hours with the other ingredients.
3. Place the cabbage and the zucchini in the last 30 minutes.
4. Serve on buns and enjoy.

Nutritional Information:
Calories: 283 kcal, Fats: 6 grams, Carbohydrates: 51 grams, Protein: 11 grams

Spicy Thai Soup

Ingredients:
1.3 liter of vegetable broth
250 ml of white whine
250 ml of water
1 yellow onion, chopped
3 green onions, chopped
4 carrots, chopped
4 stalks of celery, chopped
½ teaspoon of salt
1 teaspoon of pepper
1 tablespoon of curry powder
½ tablespoon of sage
½ teaspoon of seasoned salt
½ tablespoon of oregano
1 teaspoon of cayenne pepper
2 tablespoons of vegetable oil
1 chili pepper, seeded and chopped
1 box of rice noodles (about 150 g)

Method:
1. Chop everything up that needs to get cut up.
2. Place in the slow cooker.
3. Cook on high for around five hours or until everything is tender.
4. Serve and enjoy.

Nutritional Information:
Calories: 131 kcal, Fats: 3 grams, Carbohydrates: 14.5 grams, Protein: 7.9 grams

Lentil-Mushroom-Stew

Ingredients:
2 liter of vegetable broth
150 g of mushrooms, sliced
30 g of shiitake mushrooms, chopped
150 g of uncooked pearl barley
150 g of lentils
40 g of onion flakes
2 teaspoons of minced garlic
2 teaspoons of pepper
3 bay leaves
1 teaspoon of basil
1 teaspoon of salt

Method:
1. Cut up everything and place in slow cooker.
2. Stir well and cook on high heat for four hours.
3. Remove bay leaves.
4. Serve and enjoy.

Nutritional Information:
Calories: 213 kcal, Fats: 1.2 grams, Carbohydrates: 43.9 grams, Protein: 8.4 grams

Mexican Spaghetti with Sauce

Ingredients:
100 g of chopped onion
1 tablespoon of olive oil
900 g of meatless spaghetti sauce
1 can (about 300 g) of black beans
200 g of diced tomatoes
180 g of corn
70 g of salsa
120 g of green chilies
1 tablespoon of chili powder
¼ teaspoon of pepper
1 box of spaghetti (about 150 g)

Method:
1. Chop the onion up and cook in a skillet with the oil until they are clear.
2. In a large saucepan combine everything else together and stir well.
3. Cook on a simmer for about 20 minutes.
4. Serve sauce over spaghetti noodles and enjoy.

Nutritional Information:
Calories: 216.3 kcal, Fats: 4.8 grams, Carbohydrates: 36.1 grams, Protein: 9.0 grams

Chicken Soup

Ingredients:
3-4 chicken breasts
8 cloves fresh garlic, chopped
Low salt and freshly ground pepper, to taste
200 g cabbage, thinly shredded
1 green bell pepper, deseeded, diced
1 yellow summer squash, diced)
2 zucchini squash, cut up
6 to 8 baby potatoes, cut up
120 g chopped green chillies
1 tsp sage
1 tsp each of: dried basil, oregano, and parsley
420 g diced tomatoes
600 ml chicken broth, as needed
A dash or two of balsamic vinegar to taste
Olive oil, as needed

Method:
1. Drizzle some olive oil into a slow cooker and lay the chicken breasts in it, with half the chopped garlic. Season a little with sea salt and pepper.

2. In a bowl, combine the bell pepper, shredded cabbage, zucchini squashes, potatoes, and green chilies, tossing them with another drizzle of olive oil. Season the mixture with sea salt, black pepper, herbs and toss to coat.

3. Pour the veggie mix into the slow cooker in an even layer. Add in the tomatoes, chicken broth, and a small dash of balsamic vinegar, to taste.

4. The liquid content should just about cover the veggies in the pot. If you like, you can add more broth to get better consistency of a soup.

5. Cover the pot and let it cook for up to 5 to 6 hours, or until the chicken is tender and easily breaks apart into pieces.

Nutritional Information:
Calories: 277 kcal; Fats: 8.9g; Carbohydrates: 13.6g; Protein: 35.0g

Slow Cooked Macaroni with Cheese

Ingredients:
2 eggs
350 ml of milk
360 ml of evaporated milk
250 g of elbow macaroni
400 g of shredded cheddar cheese
1 teaspoon of salt
½ teaspoon of pepper

Method:
1. Combine everything into the slow cooker and stir well.
2. Cook on low for about five hours and stir every so often.
3. Serve and enjoy.

Nutritional Information:
Calories: 592 kcal, Fats: 33.5 grams, Carbohydrates: 39.5 grams, Protein: 32.6 grams

Turkey Stew Chilies

Ingredients:
250 g butternut squash, peeled and diced
500 g ground turkey
2 large potatoes, peeled and diced
3 medium carrots, peeled and chopped
1 onion, diced
4 cloves garlic, minced
1 tsp cumin
1 tsp chili powder
240 g roasted chopped green chili
1 liter chicken stock
Salt and black pepper to taste
For serving:
Juice from 1 lime
2-3 tbsp chopped cilantro
1-2 tsp agave nectar, as needed

Method:
1. Firstly, brown the ground pork in a skillet and take out the excess fat, if any.
2. Now add the pork to the slow cooker with the remaining ingredients up to sea salt and black pepper. Stir well to combine.
3. Cover and cook until the pork is done.
4. About 20 minutes before serving, stir in the lime juice and cilantro. Add some sweetener, if needed, to balance out the spice and if you need a little more liquid, add more broth to it and heat through.

Nutritional information:
Calories: 423 kcal; Fats: 13.5g; Carbohydrates: 44.7g; Protein: 36.3g

Crock Beans

Ingredients:
1 onion, chopped
600 g of pinto beans
30 g of chopped jalapeno pepper
2 tablespoons of minced garlic
5 teaspoons of salt
¾ teaspoons of pepper
1/8 teaspoon of cumin
2 liter of water

Method:
1. Chop up the onion and place in the slow cooker with everything else.
2. Cook on high for about five hours.
3. Once the beans are cooked, strain them and mash them.
4. Serve and enjoy.

Nutritional Information:
Calories: 139 kcal, Fats: 0.5 grams, Carbohydrates: 25.4 grams, Protein: 8.5 grams

Vegetable-Cheese-Soup

Ingredients:
550 g of creamed corn
230 g of potatoes, peeled and cubed
100 g of carrots, chopped
½ onion, chopped
1 teaspoon of celery seed
½ teaspoon of pepper
1.5 liter of vegetable broth
600 g of cheese sauce

Method:
1. Peel and chop everything then place in the slow cooker.
2. Stir well and cook on medium heat for about five hours.
3. Serve and enjoy.

Nutritional Information:
Calories: 316 kcal, Fats: 16.5 grams, Carbohydrates: 32.1 grams, Protein: 11.9 grams

Vegetable-Bean-Soup

Ingredients:
500 g of black beans
1.5 liter of water
1 carrot, chopped
1 stalk of celery, chopped
1 red onion, chopped
6 cloves of garlic, crushed
2 green bell peppers, chopped
2 jalapeno peppers, chopped
50 g of lentils
4 diced tomatoes
2 tablespoons of chili powder
2 teaspoons of ground cumin
½ teaspoon of oregano
½ teaspoon of pepper
3 tablespoons of red wine vinegar
1 tablespoon of salt
100 g of white rice

Method:
1. Chop and mince everything and then mix it all together in the slow cooker.
2. Place on high heat and cook for about three hours.
3. Serve and enjoy.

Nutritional Information:
Calories: 231 kcal, Fats: 1.2 grams, Carbohydrates: 43.4 grams, Protein: 12.6 grams

Bowtie Pasta with Sauce

Ingredients:
10 plum tomatoes, peeled and crushed
½ of an onion, chopped
1 teaspoon of garlic, minced
60 ml of olive oil
1 teaspoon of oregano
1 teaspoon of basil
1 teaspoon of cayenne pepper
1 teaspoon of salt
1 teaspoon of pepper
1 pinch of cinnamon
1 box of bowtie pasta (about 150 g)

Method:
1. Peel and crush the tomatoes, mince the garlic and chop the onion.
2. Place everything in the slow cooker and stir well.
3. Cook on high for about four hours or so.
4. Serve and enjoy.

Nutritional Information:
Calories: 105 kcal, Fats: 9.3 grams, Carbohydrates: 5.5 grams, Protein: 1.2 grams

Rice Casserole

Ingredients:
2 onions, chopped
3 stalks of celery, sliced
1 kg of mixed rice
650 ml of water
1 can (about 200 g) of mushroom soup
120 g of butter
250 g of shredded American cheese (Hard Cheese)
40 g of mushrooms, sliced

Method:
1. Chop everything up that needs to get cut and place in the slow cooker.
2. Add everything else but the cheese in the slow cooker.
3. Cook on high for about four hours.
4. Serve and enjoy with the shredded cheese on top.

Nutritional Information:
Calories: 408 kcal, Fats: 23 grams, Carbohydrates: 39.5 grams, Protein: 11.6 grams

Creamy Potato Soup

Ingredients:
1 onion, chopped
1 liter of chicken broth
500 ml of water
5 potatoes, diced
½ teaspoon of salt
½ teaspoon of dill weed
½ teaspoon of pepper
½ cup of all-purpose flour
460 g of half and half cream
360 ml of evaporated milk

Method:
1. Chop and dice everything that needs to get cut and combine all of the ingredients into the slow cooker.
2. Cook on high heat for about three and a half hours.
3. Serve and enjoy, try with some sour cream and some shredded cheese on top.

Nutritional Information:
Calories: 553 kcal, Fats: 19.3 grams, Carbohydrates: 74.2 grams, Protein: 22 grams

Slow Cooker Cassoulet

Ingredients:
500 g navy beans, dry, soaked overnight
1 liter mushroom broth
1 cube vegetable bouillon
1 onion
2 carrots, peeled and diced
1 potato, peeled and cubed
4 sprigs of parsley
1 sprig of rosemary
1 sprig of lemon thyme, chopped
1 sprig of savory
1 bay leaf
2 tbsp olive oil, extra virgin

Method:
1. In a large skillet, heat the oil over medium heat. Stir in the onion and the carrots and cook until it becomes tender.

2. In a slow cooker, combine the beans with the broth, bouillon, carrots, onion and bay leaf. Add in half a cup of water if required.

3. Season the mixture with parsley, thyme, rosemary and savory and allow it to cook on low heat for approximately 8 hours or so.

4. Next, stir in the potato and continue to cook for another hour.

5. Remove all the herbs and serve.

Nutritional Information:
Calories; 279, Fats 4.4g, Carbohydrates 47.2g, Protein 15.3g

Risotto with Fennel and Barley

Ingredients:
2 teaspoons of fennel seeds
1 fennel bulb, cored and diced
200 g of brown rice
1 carrot, chopped
1 shallot, chopped
2 cloves of garlic, minced
1 liter of chicken broth
350 ml of water
80 ml of dry white wine
300 g of green beans
50 g of shredded parmesan cheese
70 g of pitted black olives, chopped
1 tablespoon of grated lemon zest
½ teaspoon of salt
½ teaspoon of pepper

Method:
1. Chop the carrot, the shallot, the black olives and core and chop the fennel bulb.
2. Grate the lemon zest and mince the garlic.
3. Place all of the ingredients into the slow cooker and stir until well mixed.
4. Cook for three and a half hours on low.
5. Stir and cook until desired heat is cooked all the way through.
6. Serve and enjoy, try some parmesan cheese on top.

Nutritional Information:
Calories: 242 kcal, Fats: 6 grams, Carbohydrates: 36 grams, Protein: 10 grams

Slow Cooker Beans

Ingredients:
500 g of dried beans, mix pinto beans with black beans and kidney beans
1 onion, chopped
4 cloves of garlic, minced
1 teaspoon of thyme
1 bay leaf
1.3 liter of boiling water
½ teaspoon of salt

Method:
1. Place the beans in a large pot with the water, bring to a boil on high heat and cook for about one hour.
2. Drain the beans.
3. Chop the onion and mince the garlic.
4. Add to the beans and stir well.
5. Lower heat and cook for about three more hours.
6. Add the salt and cook for 15 more minutes.
7. Serve and enjoy.

Nutritional Information:
Calories: 260 kcal, Fats: 1 gram, Carbohydrates: 48 grams, Protein: 15 grams

Onion Soup

Ingredients:
6 tablespoons of butter
4 onions, sliced
1 tablespoon of white sugar
2 cloves of garlic, minced
120 ml of cooking sherry
1.7 liter of vegetable broth
1 teaspoon of salt
¼ teaspoon of thyme
1 bay leaf
8 slices of French bread
50 g of shredded parmesan cheese
40 g of shredded Colby jack cheese
30 g of cheddar cheese
2 tablespoons of mozzarella cheese

Method:
1. Chop everything up that needs to be cut and place in the slow cooker.
2. Add in everything else but the cheese and the bread.
3. Broil the bread in the oven for about three months.
4. Place the slow cooker on high heat and cook for five hours.
5. Serve and enjoy with some of the bread and the cheese on top.

Nutritional Information:
Calories: 250 kcal, Fats: 14.7 grams, Carbohydrates: 17.5 grams, Protein: 11 grams

Zucchini Soup

Ingredients:
200 g of chopped celery
1 kg of zucchini, sliced
6 tomatoes, diced
2 green bell peppers, sliced
100 g of chopped onion
2 teaspoons of salt
1 teaspoon of white sugar
1 teaspoon of oregano
1 teaspoon of Italian seasoning
1 teaspoon of basil
¼ teaspoon of garlic powder
6 tablespoons of shredded parmesan cheese

Method:
1. Chop up everything that needs to get cut up and place in the slow cooker except for the cheese.
2. Stir well and put on high heat.
3. Cook for about three and a half hours.
4. Serve and enjoy with some of the shredded cheese on top.

Nutritional Information:
Calories: 389 kcal, Fats: 23.6 grams, Carbohydrates: 25.8 grams, Protein: 21.8 grams

Lentil Soup

Ingredients:
400 g of brown lentils
750 ml of chicken broth
1 bay leaf
100 g of carrots, chopped
100 g of celery, chopped
150 g of onion, chopped
1 teaspoon of Worcestershire sauce
½ teaspoon of garlic powder
¼ teaspoon of nutmeg
5 drops of hot sauce
¼ teaspoon of caraway seed
½ teaspoon of celery salt
1 tablespoon of parsley
½ teaspoon of pepper

Method:
1. Cut up everything that needs to get cut up.
2. Place in the slow cooker and cook on high for about five hours.
3. Remove the bay leaf.
4. Serve and enjoy.

Nutritional Information:
Calories: 221 kcal, Fats: 2.3 grams, Carbohydrates: 34.2 grams, Protein: 16 grams

Veggy Taco Soup

Ingredients:
1 onion, chopped
1 can (about 300 g) of chili beans
1 can (about 300 g) of kidney beans
1 can (about 150 g) of corn
1 can (about 250 g) of tomato sauce
500 ml of water
6 tomatoes, diced
2 green chili peppers
3 tablespoons of taco seasoning mix

Method:
1. Cut up everything that needs to be diced.
2. Place in the slow cooker and stir well.
3. Cook on high for about three and a half hours.
4. Serve and enjoy, try with some sour cream and shredded cheese on top.

Nutritional Information:
Calories: 362 kcal, Fats: 16.3 grams, Carbohydrates: 37.8 grams, Protein: 18.2 grams

Cabbage Soup

Ingredients:
2 tablespoons of vegetable oil
1 onion, chopped
500 g of cabbage, chopped
500 g of red kidney beans
500 ml of water
1200 g of tomato sauce
4 tablespoons of seasoned salt
1 ½ teaspoons of cumin
1 teaspoon of salt
1 teaspoon of pepper

Method:
1. Chop the cabbage and the onion up.
2. Place in slow cooker with everything else.
3. Cook on high for four hours.
4. Serve and enjoy.

Nutritional Information:
Calories: 211 kcal, Fats: 8.7 grams, Carbohydrates: 20.3 grams, Protein: 14.1 grams

Corn Chowder

Ingredients:
5 potatoes, peeled and cubed
2 onions, chopped
3 stalks of celery, chopped
150 g of whole kernel corn
2 tablespoons of butter
½ teaspoon of salt
½ teaspoon of pepper
2 tablespoons of seasoned salt
200 ml of evaporated milk

Method:
1. Peel and cube the potatoes.
2. Chop the onions and the celery.
3. Combine everything in the slow cooker.
4. Set on high heat and cook for about four hours.
5. Serve and enjoy.

Nutritional Information:
Calories: 266 kcal, Fats: 8.8 grams, Carbohydrates: 37.8 grams, Protein: 11.2 grams

Tofu Curry

Ingredients:
500 g tofu, firm, cubed
300 g sweet corn
450 ml coconut milk
55 g curry paste
500 ml vegetable stock
180 g tomato paste
1 yellow pepper, chopped
1 red pepper, chopped
1 sweet onion, chopped
3 garlic cloves, minced
2 ginger, minced
1 tbsp garam masala
1 tsp low salt
Cilantro (for garnishing)

Method:
1. Start by cutting the tofu into ½ inch/1 cm cubes and add it to a large slow cooker.
2. Next add the chopped onion, peppers; ginger and garlic to the slow cooker as well followed by the corn, vegetable stock, tomato paste, coconut milk and spices.
3. Stir well! Then cover and allow the curry to cook on high heat for approximately 3 to 4 hours.
4. Serve over brown rice or as desired.

Nutritional Information:
Calories: 328 kcal, Fats: 7 grams, Carbohydrates: 53.8 grams, Protein: 12.8 grams

Lima Bean Soup

Ingredients:
300 g of lima beans
1 can (about 250 g) of butter beans
2 potatoes, diced
2 stalks of celery, chopped
2 onions, chopped
3 carrots, sliced
60 g of butter
½ tablespoon of diced marjoram
1 teaspoon of salt
½ teaspoon of pepper
750 ml of vegetable broth

Method:
1. Dice and cut everything that needs to be cut up.
2. Place in the slow cooker with everything else.
3. Set on high for four hours.
4. Serve and enjoy.

Nutritional Information:
Calories: 326 kcal, Fats: 11.4 grams, Carbohydrates: 43.7 grams, Protein: 13 grams

Vegetarian Soup

Ingredients:
1.5 liter of vegetable broth
4 tomatoes, diced
1 can (about 300 g) of kidney beans
1 onion, chopped
2 stalks of celery, chopped
150 g of green beans
1 zucchini, chopped
3 cloves of garlic, minced
1 tablespoon of parsley
1 ½ teaspoons of oregano
1 teaspoon of salt
¾ teaspoon of thyme
¼ teaspoon of pepper
80 g of elbow noodles
900 g of spinach, chopped
25 g of shredded parmesan cheese

Method:
1. Chop everything up that needs to get cut up.
2. Place in the slow cooker with everything but the cheese.
3. Put on high for four hours or so.
4. Serve and enjoy with the cheese on top.

Nutritional Information:
Calories: 138 kcal, Fats: 1.7 grams, Carbohydrates: 25.2 grams, Protein: 6.9 grams

Image sources/Printing information

Pictures cover: depositphotos.com;

@ Zsuriel; @annohoychuk; @zkruger; @ okkijan

Print edition black and white paperback:

Amazon Media EU S.à.r.l.

5 Rue Plaetis

L-2338 Luxembourg

Other printouts:

epubli, a service of neopubli GmbH, Berlin

Publisher:

BookRix GmbH & Co. KG

Sonnenstraße 23

80331 München

Deutschland

Printed in Great Britain
by Amazon